THE COLLEGE SUCCESS SYSTEM

How to Navigate College With Strategy, Resilience, and Purpose

By

DR. KORTNEE BURRELL

THE COLLEGE SUCCESS SYSTEM

How to Navigate College with Strategy, Resilience, and Purpose

admin@leap-resilience.com

ISBN Paperback - 979-8-218-62102-5
ISBN Hardcover - 979-8-234-07918-3

Printed in the United States.

Cover design by H. Khan

First Edition – 2026

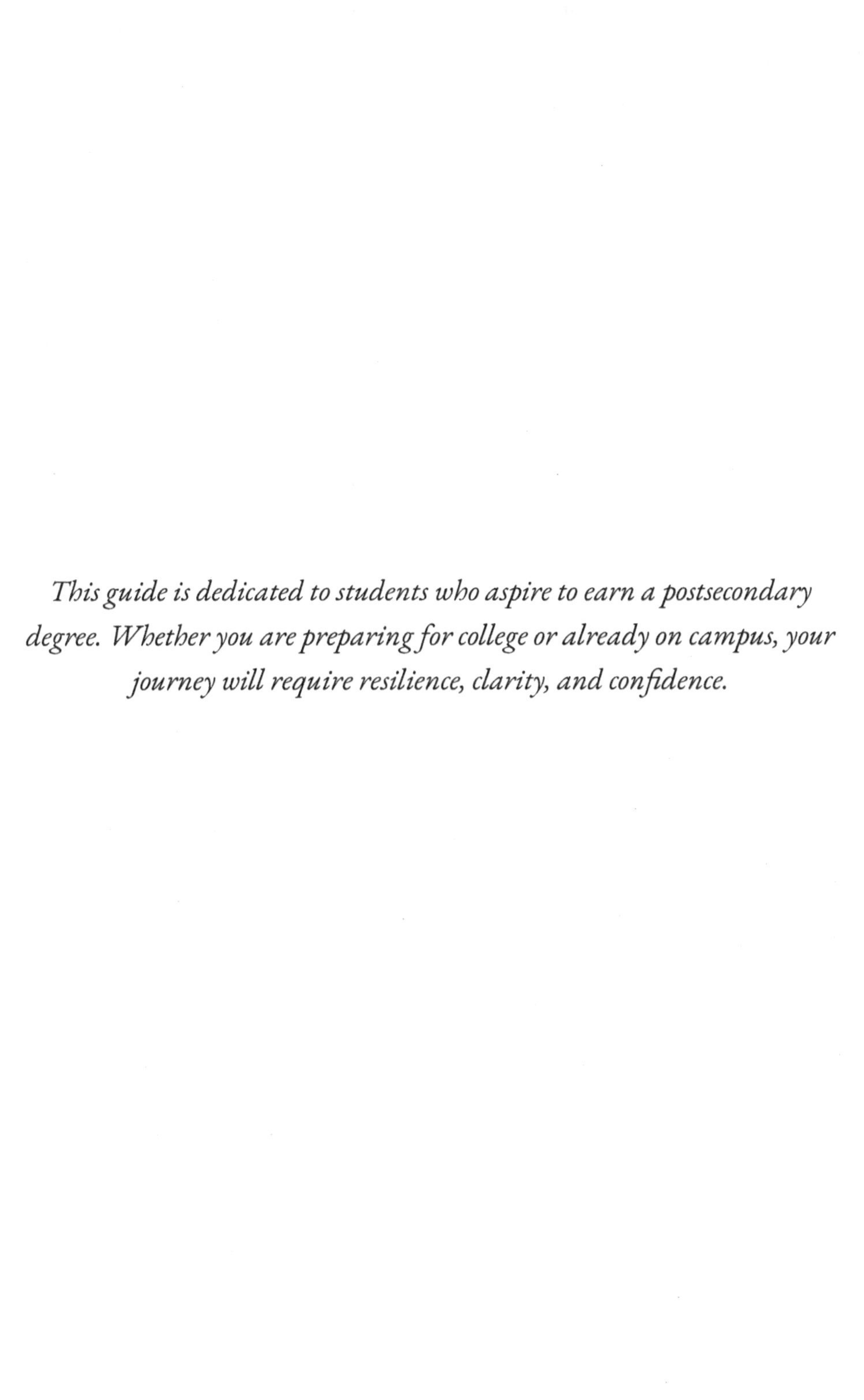

This guide is dedicated to students who aspire to earn a postsecondary degree. Whether you are preparing for college or already on campus, your journey will require resilience, clarity, and confidence.

“Successful students stay intentional, use their resources, and keep moving forward.”

– DR. KORTNEE BURRELL

PREFACE

As you begin your college journey, you may feel excited, uncertain, or even overwhelmed at times. This is completely normal. Navigating college takes time, effort, and the right support.

You may be entering this experience with confidence, or you may feel unsure about what to expect. You may be asking yourself if you are prepared, if you will be able to keep up, or if you are making the right decisions. These thoughts are more common than you think.

This guide was created to help you move through your journey with clarity and confidence. Through years of working with students in higher education, I have seen what helps students succeed and what causes them to struggle. Students are capable and motivated, but they are not always given the tools or strategies needed to thrive. This book is designed to address that gap.

College is more than attending classes and earning a degree. It is a time to grow, develop meaningful relationships, and prepare for your future. Along the way, you may face challenges with time management, academic expectations, motivation, or adjusting to a new environment. These experiences are part of the process. With the right approach, they can become opportunities for growth.

In this guide, you will find practical strategies you can apply right away. You will learn how to use campus resources, connect with professors and peers, set clear goals, and manage your time in a way that strengthens your performance and builds confidence.

Success in college is not about being perfect. Success comes from consistency, taking initiative, and continuing to move forward, even when challenges feel difficult. Guidance is available throughout your journey.

My goal is to give you a clear path to navigate college with purpose and confidence. With the right strategies and mindset, you can create a college experience that prepares you for the future you want. This guide provides those strategies and tools to support your college journey. Outcomes will vary based on individual effort, circumstances, and application of these strategies.

Wishing you success as you begin this journey.

Dr. Kortnee Burrell

YOUR COLLEGE JOURNEY

Your Name: ______________________________

Your Major: ______________________________

College Attending: ______________________________

Take a moment to write this down. This is where your journey begins.

TABLE OF CONTENTS

INTRODUCTION

The Significance of Perseverance and Dedication in College

You may begin your college journey with strong potential, but what separates you from those who succeed is how you respond to challenges, manage your time, and use the support available to you. Most importantly, college will require you to keep moving forward, even when the path ahead feels uncertain.

College: A Journey of Growth, Resilience, and Self-Discovery

College is a time to grow, develop independence, and discover who you are becoming. You may experience academic, social, or personal challenges. At times, you may feel uncertain or overwhelmed. These experiences are part of the process.

What matters is how you respond.

Students who make progress are not those who avoid challenges. They are the ones who face them, adjust their approach, and continue to move forward. Each obstacle you encounter is an opportunity to develop resilience, strengthen your mindset, and develop skills that will carry into your future.

Common Challenges Students Face in College

Students often enter college without fully understanding expectations. The transition from a structured environment to one that requires independence can feel overwhelming.

You may face challenges such as:

- Managing your time effectively
- Understanding academic expectations
- Staying motivated and consistent
- Building relationships with professors and peers
- Adjusting to a new environment

These challenges are common. They do not mean you are unprepared. They mean you are in a new phase of growth.

Successful students recognize these challenges early and take initiative. They seek support, ask questions, and make use of the resources available to them.

Purpose and Key Takeaways from this Guide

This guide was created to give you a clear path for navigating college with confidence and purpose. You will learn practical strategies that you can apply immediately to improve your academic performance, foster strong connections, and stay organized.

Throughout this book, you will learn how to:

- Use campus resources effectively
- Build a strong support network
- Develop effective study skills
- Set and achieve meaningful goals
- Manage your time with consistency and intention
- Prepare for your future beyond college

This is not about doing everything perfectly. Act, learn from your experiences, and continue to grow.

Key Insight

You have the potential to succeed in college.

With the right strategies, the right mindset, and a willingness to act, you can create a college experience that prepares you for the future you want.

Stay focused. Stay committed. Keep going.

The Leap-Resilience Student Success Framework

Success in college develops through consistent action, structured habits, and the ability to use support effectively.

The Leap-Resilience Student Success Framework provides a clear structure to help you navigate college with purpose, direction, and confidence. Each part of this framework focuses on a key area that supports your success.

When you strengthen these areas together, you improve your ability to stay on track, respond to challenges, and continue moving forward.

1. Academic Navigation

Academic navigation requires understanding how college works and making informed decisions about your education.

This includes:

- Understanding degree requirements
- Selecting courses that support your goals
- Meeting with academic advisors
- Tracking your progress toward graduation

Students who learn how to navigate the academic system early and use available guidance are more likely to stay on track.

2. Time Management

Time management focuses on how you use your time each day.

This includes:

- Planning your weekly schedule
- Prioritizing tasks and responsibilities
- Starting assignments early
- Managing deadlines with consistency

When you manage your time effectively, you reduce stress, stay organized, and improve your performance.

3. Effective Study Skills

Effective study skills focus on how you learn, understand, and apply information.

This includes:

- Using active learning strategies
- Developing consistent study habits
- Preparing for exams in advance
- Reviewing and retaining information

When you improve how you study, you improve how you perform.

4. Resilience and Adaptability

Resilience allows you to respond to challenges and continue moving forward.

This includes:

- Managing setbacks
- Staying motivated during difficult moments
- Adjusting your approach when needed
- Maintaining focus under pressure

Challenges will occur. Your response determines your progress.

5. Campus Resource Utilization

Colleges provide support systems designed to help you succeed. Using these resources strengthens your performance and builds confidence.

This includes:

- Academic advising
- Tutoring services
- Professors and office hours
- Counseling and support services

Success in college starts with one decision: taking action early.

6. Career and Future Planning

Your college experience should prepare you for what comes next.

This includes:

- Exploring career options
- Learning relevant skills
- Gaining internships and experience
- Connecting with career advisors

Planning early helps you make decisions that support your long-term goals.

How to Use This Framework

Each chapter in this guide helps you strengthen one or more areas of this framework.

You do not need to master everything at once. Focus on consistent progress, apply what you've learned, and continue strengthening each area over time.

Key Insight

Your success is not determined by a single decision or a single moment.

It develops through the actions you take, the habits you build, and the support you choose to embrace.

Now that you understand the importance of perseverance, structure, and using available support, the next step is learning how to take action. In Chapter 1, you will learn how to use on-campus resources to support your success and build a strong foundation for your college journey.

CHAPTER 1
Connect with On-Campus Resources

"Successful students act with intention and use their campus resources."

— DR. KORTNEE BURRELL

Entering college is an exciting step, but it also requires adjustment. You are expected to manage your time, stay organized, and take responsibility for your learning. It is common for students to struggle not because they lack ability, but because they do not use the resources available to them.

You may believe you need to figure everything out on your own, but you were never meant to do this alone. This often leads to unnecessary stress and missed opportunities for support.

Every college provides support systems designed to help you succeed. These include academic advising, tutoring, counseling services, and career support. The students who take advantage of these resources early are the ones who gain confidence, perform better academically, and stay on track.

Using campus resources is not a sign that you are struggling. It is a sign that you are taking ownership of your success.

Why Campus Resources Matter

College is different from high school. You are expected to have independence, and support is not always brought to you. You must seek support.

When you use campus resources, you:

- Gain clarity when you feel unsure
- Strengthen your understanding of course material
- Develop relationships with people who can support your growth
- Position yourself for long-term success

Successful students don't wait until they're overwhelmed. They connect with campus resources early and stay consistent.

Student Example

During her first semester, Jasmine struggled in her biology course. She attended lectures and completed assignments, but her exam scores were lower than expected. Rather than continuing to struggle, she visited the tutoring center and attended her professor's office hours.

At first, Jasmine felt unsure about asking for help. However, after a few sessions at the tutoring center and attending her professor's office hours, she began to understand the material more clearly and learned how to study more effectively. By the end of the semester, her grades improved, and her confidence in her ability to succeed grew.

Jasmine's experience is not unique. The difference was not intelligence. It was her decision to use the resources available to her.

Student Example (Continued)

Sanjay entered college confident in his abilities. In high school, he performed well without needing much support, so he assumed college would be the same. During his first semester, he managed his coursework on his own and avoided reaching out for help.

As the semester progressed, Sanjay found himself falling behind. His assignments became more demanding, and he struggled to keep up with deadlines. Instead of continuing to push through on his own, he decided to meet with an academic advisor and visit the campus learning center.

During his advising session, Sanjay realized he had been taking on too much at once. His advisor helped him adjust his schedule and create a plan for managing his workload. At the learning center, he learned time management strategies that helped him stay organized and focused.

By the end of the semester, Sanjay was no longer overwhelmed. He had a system in place, a clearer plan, and the confidence to ask for help.

Sanjay's success came from recognizing that independence does not mean doing everything alone. It means knowing when to use the support available to you.

Key Campus Resources to Use

Academic Advising

Academic advisors help you:

- Choose the right courses
- Stay on track toward graduation
- Explore majors and career paths

Meeting with your advisor regularly helps you make informed decisions and avoid delays in your progress.

Professors and Office Hours

Your professors are one of your most valuable resources.

You can:

- Ask questions about course material
- Seek clarification on assignments
- Get guidance on academic and career goals

Developing relationships with professors can lead to mentorship, recommendations, and future opportunities.

Familiarizing yourself with the resources available on your campus and using them makes all the difference.

Taking Action: Start the Conversation

One of the most effective steps you can take is starting a conversation with your professors or academic advisor. You do not need to have everything figured out. You just need to be willing to ask questions and seek clarity.

If you are not sure where to begin, start by asking simple questions such as:

- What is the best way to succeed in this course?
- How should I prepare for exams and assignments?
- What courses should I take next semester?
- How can I improve my performance?

These conversations can give you direction, improve your confidence, and help you make better decisions.

A full list of guided questions to help you engage with academic advisors, professors, and career services is included at the end of this book.

Tutoring Services

Tutoring is available to support your learning in specific subjects.

It can help you:

- Strengthen your understanding
- Improve study strategies
- Prepare for exams

Tutoring is not just for students who are struggling. It is for any student who wants to improve.

Counseling and Mental Health Services

College life challenges you in new ways. Taking care of your mental well-being is part of your success.

Counseling services can help you:

- Manage pressure and stay focused
- Cultivate self-awareness
- Navigate personal challenges

Seeking support is a proactive step toward maintaining your overall well-being.

Common Mistakes to Avoid

- Waiting too long to ask for help
- Trying to manage everything on your own
- Ignoring available campus resources
- Only seeking support after falling behind
- Assuming asking for help is a weakness

Key Insight

You do not have to figure everything out on your own.

The support you need is already available.

Reflection and Application

Take a moment to reflect and apply what you have learned.

Reflection Questions

1. What campus resources are you currently using, and how are they helping you succeed?
2. What is one resource you have not used yet that could support your progress?
3. What is one action you can take this week to seek academic or personal support?
4. Who is one person on campus you can connect with for guidance or mentorship?

Student Action Checklist

Start with taking the following actions:

- ☐ Schedule a meeting with an academic advisor.
- ☐ Attend one professor's office hour.
- ☐ Visit one campus resource (tutoring, counseling, or career center).
- ☐ Introduce yourself to one staff member or faculty member.
- ☐ Write down one question and get it answered.

Notes

Use this space to write key ideas, insights, or next steps.

In Chapter 1, you learned how to use campus resources to support your academic and personal success. While these resources provide valuable support, the relationships you build with professors, advisors, and peers play an equally important role. In Chapter 2, you will learn how to build a strong network of support that helps you stay motivated, gain guidance, and move forward with confidence.

CHAPTER 2
Build a Network of Support

"Students are more likely to succeed when they build strong connections and use the support around them."

— DR. KORTNEE BURRELL

College is not meant to be navigated alone. While independence is important, success is often built through the relationships you develop along the way.

It is common for students to focus only on their coursework and overlook one of the most important parts of their success: the people around them.

Trying to manage everything alone can lead to isolation, stress, and missed opportunities.

Strong students are intentional about developing relationships with professors, advisors, peers, and mentors who can support their growth.

The relationships you develop will influence your experience, your confidence, and your future.

Why Building a Support Network Matters

A strong support system can help you:

- Stay motivated during challenging moments
- Gain advice and direction when you feel uncertain
- Learn from others' experiences
- Access opportunities you may not find on your own

Students who build connections early are more likely to feel confident, supported, and prepared.

Key Relationships to Build

Professors and Faculty

Professors can offer:

- Academic guidance
- Career insight
- Mentorship
- Letters of recommendation

Building relationships with professors helps you gain support beyond the classroom.

Academic Advisors

Advisors help you:

- Plan your courses
- Stay on track toward graduation
- Explore career options

Meeting regularly with your advisor ensures you are making informed decisions.

Career Advisors

Career advisors can help you:

- Explore career paths
- Prepare for internships and jobs
- Build your resume and professional skills

Meeting with a career advisor early can help you connect your college experience to your future goals.

Peers and Classmates

Your peers can:

- Support your learning
- Provide accountability
- Share different perspectives

Joining study groups and participating in class discussions can strengthen your understanding and build connections.

Student Organizations and Campus Communities

Getting involved allows you to:

- Meet like-minded students
- Develop leadership skills
- Gain confidence
- Expand your network

These experiences often lead to opportunities both during and after college.

Student Example

During her first year, Addison focused primarily on her coursework. She attended classes, completed assignments, and studied on her own. While she performed well academically, she often felt disconnected and unsure about her direction.

One day, she decided to attend a campus event hosted by a student organization related to her major. There, she met other students with similar interests and connected with a faculty advisor who encouraged her to get involved.

Over time, Addison built relationships with peers and mentors who supported her academic and personal growth. She gained new opportunities, including leadership roles and internships.

Her college experience changed for the better once she realized that working hard matters, but building the right connections makes the difference.

Student Example (Continued)

Daniel entered college determined to succeed but kept to himself. He avoided group work when possible and did not engage much with classmates or professors.

As his courses became more demanding, he found it difficult to keep up. Instead of continuing to work in isolation, he joined a study group recommended by one of his classmates.

Through that group, Daniel was able to better understand course material, stay accountable, and build new friendships. He also became more comfortable asking questions and participating in discussions.

Daniel's experience shows that building connections can improve both academic performance and confidence.

Student Example: Academic Advisor

During her first year, Jennifer felt unsure about her course schedule. She selected classes based on what seemed manageable, but she did not fully understand how they connected to her degree requirements.

After speaking with her academic advisor, she realized she had missed an important prerequisite for her major. Her advisor helped her adjust her schedule and create a degree plan for the next few semesters.

That one meeting gave Jennifer direction. She understood what courses to take, how to stay on track, and how to avoid delays in graduation.

Jennifer's experience shows that meeting with an academic advisor early helps you make informed decisions and move forward with confidence.

Student Example: Career Advisor

During his second year, John was unsure about his career path. He was doing well in his classes, but he did not know how his major connected to future opportunities.

He decided to meet with a career advisor. During the meeting, John learned about different career options, internship opportunities, and skills employers were looking for in his field.

The career advisor helped John update his resume and encouraged him to attend a career fair. Through this meaningful experience, John secured an internship that provided real-world experience and a clearer sense of direction.

John's experience shows that meeting with a career advisor can help you connect your education to your future and take meaningful steps toward your goals.

Taking Action: Build Your Network

Building a support system does not require perfection. It starts with small steps.

Take action by:

- Introducing yourself to a classmate
- Attending a campus event
- Participating in a study group
- Reaching out to a professor or advisor

Each connection you make strengthens your support system.

Common Mistakes to Avoid

- Isolating yourself instead of building connections
- Avoiding group work or collaboration
- Not engaging with professors or classmates
- Waiting for others to initiate relationships
- Underestimating the value of a support network

Key Insight

You are not meant to do this alone.

The relationships you develop in college can shape your experience, your confidence, and your future. Stay open, stay engaged, and continue building connections that support your growth.

Reflection and Application

Take a moment to reflect and apply what you have learned.

Reflection Questions

1. Who are three people you can intentionally build a connection with this semester?
2. What is one step you can take this week to strengthen an existing relationship?
3. How comfortable are you asking for help, and what may be holding you back?

Student Action Checklist

Take the following actions this week:

- ☐ Introduce yourself to at least one classmate.
- ☐ Reach out to one professor, advisor, or mentor.
- ☐ Attend one campus event or organization meeting.
- ☐ Join or participate in a study group.
- ☐ Ask for help or clarification in one area.

Notes

Use this space to write key ideas, insights, or next steps.

In Chapter 2, you learned how to build a strong network of support through meaningful connections. With the right people around you, the next step is learning how to manage your time effectively. In Chapter 3, you will learn how to use your time with intention, stay organized, and create a structure that supports your success.

CHAPTER 3
Master Time Management

"Success with time management comes from creating intentional structure and consistently using the systems designed to support your goals."

– DR. KORTNEE BURRELL

Time is one of your most valuable resources in college. How you use it will directly affect your results. It is common for students to struggle with time management, not because they lack motivation, but because they lack a clear structure for how to use their time effectively. Managing your time is not about doing more, but about using your time with intention.

Key Strategies to Manage Your Time Effectively:

Be Intentional with Your Time

Instead of saying, "I will study more," say,

"I will study for one hour each day."

Break Your Time into Manageable Blocks

Large goals can feel overwhelming. Break them into smaller, manageable actions.

Use Deadlines to Stay on Track

Deadlines help you stay accountable and avoid procrastination.

Track How You Use Your Time

Keep a list or journal to monitor your goals and adjust when needed.

Build Consistent Time Habits

Consistency is more important than perfection. Focus on steady progress.

Example:
A student who wants to improve their performance in a course may set a clear goal such as studying for one hour each day, reviewing notes after every lecture, and completing assignments at least two days before they are due.

Instead of relying on motivation, the student follows a structured plan that supports consistent progress and reduces last-minute stress.

Taking Action: Build Your Routine

Students often struggle not because they lack ability, but because they lack structure. Without structure, it becomes harder to stay organized, manage responsibilities, and follow through consistently.

Creating a routine helps you stay organized and focused.

You can start by:

- Writing down your weekly priorities
- Scheduling time for studying and assignments
- Reviewing your progress at the end of each week

A simple routine can help you stay on track and reduce uncertainty.

Common Mistakes to Avoid

- Waiting until the last minute to begin important tasks
- Creating a schedule but not following it consistently
- Underestimating how long assignments will take
- Filling your time without setting clear priorities
- Confusing being busy with being productive

Key Insight

The way you manage your time will shape your outcomes more than any single assignment or exam.

Reflection and Application

Take a moment to reflect and apply what you have learned.

Reflection Questions

How are you currently managing your time each week?
What is one area where you tend to lose time or fall behind?

What is one change you can make to improve your daily routine?
What is one action you can take today to stay more organized and consistent?

Student Action Checklist

Apply the following steps:

- ☐ Write out your full weekly schedule.
- ☐ Block dedicated time for studying and assignments.
- ☐ Identify one distraction and reduce or remove it.
- ☐ Start one assignment earlier than usual.
- ☐ Review your week and adjust your schedule.

Notes

Use this space to write key ideas, insights, or next steps.

In Chapter 3, you learned how to manage your time and create a structure for your daily responsibilities. Managing your time is essential, but how you use that time to learn is just as important. In Chapter 4, you will learn how to develop effective study skills that improve your understanding, retention, and performance.

CHAPTER 4
Develop Effective Study Skills

"The students who succeed are the ones who learn how to study with intention and use strategies that help them understand and apply what they learn."

— DR. KORTNEE BURRELL

A common misconception is that studying longer leads to better results. However, how you study matters more than how long you study. If you have spent hours studying and still felt unprepared, you are not alone.

College-level coursework requires a different approach to learning. You may enter college using the same study habits that worked in high school. Over time, you may need to adjust your approach to meet the demands of college-level work.

Success in college is not based on studying longer. It is based on studying with intention, using strategies that help you understand, retain, and apply information.

Effective learners focus on understanding, not just memorization. They learn how to engage with their coursework, stay organized, and prepare in a way that develops confidence and consistency. When you change how you study, you change how you perform.

Why Study Skills Matter

Effective study skills help you:

- Understand course material more clearly
- Retain information over time
- Prepare for exams with confidence
- Reduce stress and last-minute cramming
- Improve overall academic performance

Without strong study skills, it is easy to feel overwhelmed or fall behind. With the right approach, you can stay in control of your learning.

Student Example

During her first semester, Elizabeth spent hours studying but struggled to perform well on exams. She reread her notes, reviewed slides, and tried to memorize information, but she often forgot what she studied.

After speaking with her professor, Elizabeth realized she needed to change her approach. Instead of passively reviewing material, she began using active study techniques. She practiced explaining concepts in her own words, tested herself regularly, and focused on understanding rather than memorizing.

Over time, Elizabeth noticed a difference. She retained more information, felt more confident during exams, and improved her performance.

Elizabeth's success came from changing how she studied, not just how long she studied.

Student Example (Continued)

William believed that studying meant waiting until the night before an exam and reviewing as much material as possible. This approach left him feeling stressed and unprepared.

After receiving feedback from his instructor, William began spreading his study sessions throughout the week. He reviewed notes after each class, completed practice questions, and used a planner to stay organized.

By the time his next exam arrived, he felt more prepared and less overwhelmed. His performance improved, and he gained confidence in his ability to manage his coursework.

William's experience shows that consistency is more effective than last-minute effort.

Key Study Skills to Develop

Active Learning

Active learning means engaging with the material instead of simply reviewing it.

You can practice active learning by:

- Explaining concepts in your own words
- Asking questions while you study
- Teaching the material to someone else
- Completing practice problems

Effective Notetaking

Your notes should help you understand and review key concepts.

Strong notetaking includes:

- Writing down main ideas instead of copying everything
- Organizing information clearly
- Reviewing and updating your notes after class

Reading for Understanding

College reading requires focus and intention.

Instead of reading passively:

- Identify key ideas and concepts
- Take notes while reading
- Pause to reflect on what you learned

Preparing for Exams

Effective exam preparation starts early.

You can prepare by:

- Reviewing material consistently
- Practicing with sample questions
- Identifying areas where you need more understanding
- Avoiding last-minute cramming

Staying Organized

Organization helps you stay on track and reduce stress.

You can stay organized by:

- Keeping track of assignments and deadlines

- Using a planner or calendar
- Breaking tasks into smaller steps

Taking Action: Improve Your Study Approach

You do not need to change everything at once. Start with taking small adjustments.

Focus first on:

- Reviewing your notes after each class
- Studying in focused blocks of time
- Testing yourself on key concepts
- Creating a study plan for the week

Consistent effort over time leads to stronger results.

Common Mistakes to Avoid

- Relying only on rereading notes
- Waiting until the last minute to study
- Studying without a clear plan
- Focusing on memorization instead of understanding
- Avoiding difficult material

Key Insight

Effective studying is not about doing more.

It is about doing what works.

When you use the right strategies and stay consistent, you build confidence in your ability to learn and succeed.

Reflection and Application

Take a moment to reflect and apply what you have learned.

Reflection Questions

1. What study habits are currently helping you succeed?
2. What study habits need improvement?
3. How do you typically prepare for exams, and is it effective?
4. What is one change you can make to improve how you study?

Student Action Checklist

Strengthen your approach with these actions:

- ☐ Review your notes after each class.
- ☐ Use one active learning strategy (practice questions, teaching, or self-testing).
- ☐ Create a study plan for the week.
- ☐ Study in focused time blocks.
- ☐ Identify one concept you need help with and seek support.

Notes

Use this space to write key ideas, insights, or next steps.

In Chapter 4, you learned how to study with intention and use strategies that improve how you learn. With these skills in place, the next step is learning how to stay focused and consistent. In Chapter 5, you will learn how to set short-term goals that help you stay organized, build momentum, and make steady progress.

CHAPTER 5
Establish Short-Term Goals

"Success in college is built through consistent effort and clear, intentional goals."

— DR. KORTNEE BURRELL

You may have goals, but goals alone are not enough without a clear plan. College success does not happen all at once. It is built over time through small, consistent actions. Without structure, even the most motivated students can fall behind.

Short-term goals help you stay focused, organized, and motivated. They break larger ambitions into manageable steps and provide a clear sense of direction in your daily work.

Successful students do not rely on motivation alone. They create structure, set clear goals, and follow through.

Why Short-Term Goals Matter

Short-term goals help you:

- Stay focused on the task in front of you
- Manage your time more effectively

- Track your progress
- Build confidence through small wins

Without clear goals, it is easy to fall behind or lose direction. When you set short-term goals, you give yourself a clear path forward.

Student Example

During his first semester, Mohammed felt overwhelmed by his workload. He had multiple assignments, exams, and responsibilities, but no clear system for managing them. He often waited until the last minute to complete his work, which affected his performance.

After receiving a low grade on an exam, Mohammed decided to change his approach. Instead of focusing only on the outcome, he began setting small, weekly goals. He created a schedule that included time for studying, reviewing notes, and completing assignments early.

Over time, Mohammed became more organized and consistent. His grades improved, and he felt more in control of his workload.

Mohammed's success came from breaking large goals into smaller, manageable steps.

Student Example (Continued)

Sofia entered college with clear long-term goals, including graduating with her degree, building a career in her field, and securing a stable future after college, but she struggled to stay consistent. She would start the semester strong academically, staying organized and on top of her assignments, but lost focus on her coursework as the workload increased and began to miss deadlines.

To stay on track toward her long-term goals, Sofia began setting daily and weekly goals. She wrote down specific tasks, such as reviewing lecture notes, completing readings, and preparing for upcoming assignments.

By focusing on daily priorities, she stayed on track and avoided falling behind. Sofia's consistency built her confidence, sustained steady progress throughout the semester, and earned her stronger grades and a sense of accomplishment.

Sofia's experience shows that success does not come from doing everything at once. It comes from showing up consistently and following through.

Types of Short-Term Goals

Academic Goals

- Complete assigned readings before class
- Review notes after each lecture
- Prepare for exams in advance
- Attend office hours when needed

Personal Development Goals

- Create a daily or weekly schedule
- Limit distractions during study time
- Improve time management habits
- Build consistent routines

Career-Oriented Goals

- Attend a career event or workshop
- Build or update your resume
- Connect with professionals in your field
- Explore internship opportunities

Taking Action: Strengthen Your Short-Term Goals

Start taking the initiative by:

- Writing down your goals for the week
- Breaking larger tasks into smaller steps
- Scheduling time to complete each task
- Reviewing your progress regularly

Small, consistent actions will help you stay focused and move forward with confidence.

Common Mistakes to Avoid

- Setting goals that are too broad or unclear
- Waiting until the last minute to complete tasks
- Relying on motivation instead of structure
- Not tracking your progress
- Trying to do too much at once

Key Insight

Short-term goals create momentum.

Momentum is built through consistent action, not occasional effort.

Focusing on today's priorities and staying consistent builds progress over time and moves you closer to your long-term goals.

Reflection and Application

Take a moment to reflect and apply what you have learned.

Reflection Questions

1. What are three specific goals you want to accomplish this week?
2. How will you track your progress toward these goals?
3. What is one obstacle that may affect your consistency?
4. What is one step you can take today to move forward?

Student Action Checklist

Focus on the following priorities:

- ☐ Write down three specific goals for the week.
- ☐ Break each goal into smaller steps.
- ☐ Schedule time to complete each step.
- ☐ Track your progress daily or weekly.
- ☐ Reflect on what worked and what needs improvement.

Notes

Use this space to write key ideas, insights, or next steps.

In Chapter 5, you learned how to set short-term goals that help you stay focused and consistent. While short-term goals support your daily progress, long-term goals give your college experience direction and purpose. In Chapter 6, you will learn how to establish long-term goals and make decisions that align with your future.

CHAPTER 6
Establish Long-Term Goals

"Long-term success is built when you stay committed to your vision and make decisions that align with your future."

— DR. KORTNEE BURRELL

It is easy to focus only on what is in front of you. Without a clear direction, it becomes difficult to make decisions that support your future. Long-term goals give your college experience direction and purpose, but they require action to become real.

You may enter college with general ideas about what you want, such as graduating, finding a job, or continuing your education. Without clear long-term goals, it becomes easy to lose focus or make decisions that do not support your future.

Long-term goals help you stay intentional. They guide your choices, shape your habits, and give meaning to the work you are doing now.

Why Long-Term Goals Matter

Long-term goals help you:

- Stay focused on your future

- Make better academic and career decisions
- Stay motivated during challenges
- Connect your daily work to a larger purpose

Example:

A student with a clear goal of working in healthcare may stay more focused in their courses, seek relevant experiences, and remain motivated during challenging moments because they understand how their daily work connects to their future.

Student Example:

During her second year of college, Maria realized she was unsure about her future. She was attending classes and completing assignments, but she had not thought deeply about her long-term goals.

After meeting with her academic advisor, Maria began exploring different career paths related to her major. She attended career workshops, spoke with professors, and researched opportunities in her field.

Over time, she identified a career path that aligned with her interests. With that clarity, she began selecting courses, internships, and experiences that supported her goals.

Maria's experience changed when she became intentional about her future.

Student Example (Continued)

Ethan entered college with a clear goal of attending graduate school, but he did not fully understand what it would take to get there.

After speaking with a professor, Ethan learned about the importance of maintaining a strong GPA, gaining research experience, and building relationships with faculty.

He began to plan ahead, adjusting his study habits, seeking research opportunities, and staying consistent in his coursework.

By the time he applied to graduate programs, he felt prepared and confident in his qualifications. He earned acceptance into the graduate program of his choice.

Student Example: Changing Direction

During her first year, Jessica chose a major based on what she thought was practical, not what truly interested her. She enrolled in courses based on her academic plan but often felt disconnected from her classes and unsure about her future.

After taking time to reflect and speak with her advisor, Jessica realized her interests aligned more with a different field. She made the decision to change her major and began exploring new opportunities that matched her strengths.

Although switching majors required adjustment, Jessica became more engaged in her coursework, gained a clearer sense of direction, and felt more confident in her future.

Jessica's experience shows that choosing a major aligned with your interests can increase engagement, build confidence, and provide a clearer sense of direction.

Student Example: Starting Late

During his early college years, Sebastian focused only on completing his classes without thinking about what would come after graduation. He assumed he would figure out everything later.

As he approached his final year, he realized he had not gained experience related to his field. He had no internships, limited connections, and little clarity about his next steps.

Instead of becoming discouraged, Sebastian took the initiative. He met with a career advisor, attended networking events, and began applying for opportunities. Although he started later than he expected, he was able to gain experience and move forward with a clearer plan.

Sebastian's experience shows that it is never too late to take ownership of your future. However, starting early gives you more time and more options.

Long-term goals can take different forms depending on your interests, direction, and personal growth.

Types of Long-Term Goals

Academic Goals

- Graduate on time
- Maintain a strong GPA
- Complete advanced coursework or research

Example:
A student who wants to attend graduate school may focus on maintaining a strong GPA, building relationships with professors, and gaining research experience throughout college.

Career Goals

- Secure internships related to your field
- Build professional experience
- Develop skills needed for your future career

Example:
A student interested in business may begin attending networking events, securing internships, and developing professional skills early to prepare for a career after graduation.

Personal Growth Goals

- Build confidence and independence
- Strengthen communication and leadership skills
- Develop discipline and consistency

Example:
A student who wants to build confidence may join a student organization, take on leadership roles, and challenge themselves to step outside of their comfort zone.

Long-term goals become meaningful when they are supported by consistent action and intentional decisions.

Turning Long-Term Goals into Actionable Goals

Long-term goals only matter if you take steps toward them.

Example:
A student who wants to become a teacher may begin by selecting an education major, completing required coursework, gaining classroom experience through internships, and building relationships with mentors in the field. Each step moves them closer to achieving their long-term goal.

Break Goals Into Smaller Milestones

Large goals become manageable when you divide them into steps.

Example:
If your long-term goal is to attend medical school, your milestones may include completing prerequisite courses, preparing for entrance exams, gaining clinical experience, and maintaining a strong academic record each semester.

Additional Example:
If your goal is to graduate on time, your milestones may include meeting with your advisor each semester, selecting the correct courses, and tracking your progress toward degree requirements.

Make Intentional Decisions

Choose courses, activities, and opportunities that support your future.

Example:
A student interested in a career in technology may choose courses, projects, and internships that build technical skills and align with their future goals, rather than choosing options simply because they are easier or more convenient.

Seek Guidance

Professors, advisors, and mentors can help you refine your goals and stay on track.

Example:
A student unsure about their career path may meet with an academic advisor to review their academic plan, explore potential majors, and identify next steps such as internships or relevant courses.

Stay Flexible

Your goals may change as you grow. Adjust your plans while staying focused on your progress.

Example:
A student may begin college planning to become a doctor but later discover a passion for public health that better aligns with their interests and strengths. They adjust their goals by changing their major, enrolling in public health

courses, and pursuing internships with community health organizations. This shift allows them to move forward with greater clarity and confidence.

Taking Action: Plan Your Future

You can begin planning your long-term goals by:

- Identifying your academic interests to clarify your path
- Researching potential career paths
- Speaking with advisors or mentors
- Setting milestones for each semester

Planning ahead helps you move forward with clarity and confidence.

Example:
A student interested in law may begin by researching legal careers, speaking with professionals, and identifying the courses and experiences needed to move forward. These steps help turn a general interest into a clear and actionable plan.

Common Mistakes to Avoid

- Not thinking about long-term goals early
- Making decisions without considering future impact
- Avoiding conversations about career planning
- Setting goals without a clear plan
- Not seeking guidance when unsure

Key Insight

Your future is shaped by the decisions you make today.

Stay focused on your goals. Make intentional choices. Continue building toward the future you want.

Reflection and Application

Take a moment to reflect and apply what you have learned.

Reflection Questions

1. What are your long-term academic or career goals?
2. What actions can you take this semester to move closer to those goals?
3. Who can you reach out to for guidance or mentorship in your field of interest?
4. How do your current habits support or limit your future goals?

Student Action Checklist

Take the next steps toward your future:

- ☐ Write down one long-term goal or direction you are interested in exploring, even if you are still unsure.
- ☐ Identify three steps you can take this semester to move closer to your goals.
- ☐ Meet with a professor, advisor, or mentor to discuss your goals and next steps.
- ☐ Research one opportunity related to your interests or future direction.
- ☐ Review your current habits and make one adjustment to support your progress.

Notes

Use this space to write key ideas, insights, or next steps.

In Chapter 6, you learned how to establish long-term goals and align your decisions with your future. As you continue working toward your goals, it is important to take time to reflect on your journey. In Chapter 7, you will learn how to recognize your progress, learn from your experiences, and continue moving forward with confidence.

CHAPTER 7
Reflections and Rewards

"Growth in college is not only measured by what you achieve, but by who you become along the way."

– DR. KORTNEE BURRELL

College is a journey filled with challenges, progress, and change. As you move forward, take time to reflect on your experiences and recognize your growth.

Success is not only about grades, accomplishments, or milestones. It also reflects the discipline you develop, the challenges you overcome, and the confidence you build.

Reflection allows you to understand your progress by identifying what worked, what didn't, and how your habits have changed over time.

Why Reflection Matters

Taking time to reflect helps you:

- Recognize your progress over time
- Learn from your experiences
- Build confidence in your abilities
- Make more informed decisions over time

Students who reflect are more aware, more intentional, and more prepared for future challenges.

Real Student Example

During her final year, Naomi began to look back on her college experience. She remembered the moments when she felt uncertain, struggled to manage multiple assignments, and questioned her ability to succeed after receiving lower exam grades. She also recognized how much she had grown. She had developed consistent study habits, learned how to manage her time effectively, built strong relationships with professors and peers, and gained confidence in her abilities. By reflecting on her journey, Naomi was able to appreciate her progress and move forward with a clearer sense of direction and confidence.

Real Student Example (Continued)

Trevor focused heavily on his academic goals throughout college. He maintained a consistent study schedule, completed assignments on time, and worked hard to meet expectations, but he rarely took time to acknowledge his progress.

After completing a major research project, one of his professors encouraged him to reflect on how far he had come. Trevor recognized that he had developed stronger study habits, improved his time management, and gained confidence in his ability to handle challenging coursework. This reflection helped him see his growth more clearly and approach his future with a stronger sense of purpose and confidence.

Trevor's experience shows that recognizing your progress plays an important role in success.

Recognizing Your Progress

While taking consistent action is essential, recognizing your progress is just as important.

Your progress in college may include:

- Becoming more independent in managing your responsibilities
- Improving your time management skills
- Strengthening your academic skills
- Building meaningful relationships with peers and mentors
- Developing confidence and resilience through challenges

Progress is not always obvious in the moment. It becomes clear when you take time to reflect.

Celebrating Your Progress

Recognizing your achievements helps you stay motivated and confident.

You can celebrate your progress by:

- Acknowledging your accomplishments
- Sharing your success with others
- Taking time to appreciate your effort
- Setting new goals for continued growth

Celebrating your progress reinforces the habits that helped you succeed.

Taking Action: Reflect and Move Forward

You can begin reflecting on your journey by:

- Writing down your experiences and lessons learned
- Identifying challenges you have overcome
- Recognizing the habits that helped you succeed
- Setting new goals based on your personal evolution

Reflection is not about looking back with regret. It is about moving forward with clarity and confidence.

Common Mistakes to Avoid

- Not taking time to reflect on your growth
- Focusing only on what went wrong
- Overlooking progress and achievements
- Comparing your journey to others
- Moving forward without learning from past experiences

Key Insight

Your college journey is shaping who you are becoming. Recognize your growth, learn from your experiences, and continue moving forward with purpose and confidence.

Reflection and Application

Take a moment to reflect and apply what you have learned.

Reflection Questions

1. What is one challenge you faced, and how did you overcome it?
2. What are you most proud of accomplishing?
3. How have you grown academically, personally, or professionally?
4. What lessons will you carry forward into your next chapter?

Student Action Checklist

This week, commit to the following actions:

- ☐ Write down three accomplishments you are proud of.
- ☐ Identify one lesson you learned from a challenge.
- ☐ Set one goal for your next phase.
- ☐ Share your progress with someone you trust.
- ☐ Celebrate one achievement, big or small.

Notes

Use this space to write key ideas, insights, or next steps.

In Chapter 7, you learned how to reflect on your experiences and recognize your growth. Reflection helps you understand your progress, but the next step is continuing to move forward. In this final section, you will bring everything together and focus on taking action with purpose and confidence.

CONCLUSION
Keep Moving Forward

Even if you do not have everything figured out, you can still move forward. Uncertainty will show up. Plans will shift. Doubt may appear. At times, you may feel behind or question your progress.

Keep going.

Success in college does not come from perfection. It does not come from having all the answers or avoiding mistakes.
Success is built through action, consistency, and the decision to keep moving forward during challenging moments.

Throughout this guide, you learned how to:

- Use your resources with intention
- Build meaningful connections
- Manage your time effectively
- Strengthen how you learn
- Set goals that support your future

Now the next step belongs to you.

Start now.
Take one step.
Then take another.

Progress may not show up immediately, but every action builds something greater.
You build discipline. You strengthen your confidence. You begin to shape your future.

College goes beyond earning a degree.
College shapes who you become.

You grow into someone who leads with focus, resilience, and purpose.

You already have the foundation to move forward and succeed.
Even on the days when doubt shows up, you still have what it takes.
Even when the path ahead feels uncertain, you can keep moving forward.

Stay focused.
Stay consistent.
Keep moving forward.

Your future does not wait.
You shape your future.

Visualization: Imagine Your Future

Imagine your name.
Imagine your degree.
Imagine the moment your hard work becomes reality.

My Name:

____

My Degree:

____

Now act with purpose and take steps toward earning your degree.

APPENDIX

Questions to Ask Academic Advisors, Professors, and Career Advisors

---

How to Use This Section

This appendix is designed to help you take meaningful action. Use these questions to guide your conversations, gain clarity, and make informed decisions throughout your college journey.

You do not need to ask every question at once. Start by asking a few questions, show confidence, and continue using this section as a resource throughout your time in college.

Questions to Ask an Academic Advisor

Academic advisors help you stay on track, make informed decisions, and plan your path toward graduation. Meeting with your advisor regularly can help you avoid mistakes and move forward with clarity.

Start by asking questions such as:

- What courses should I take next semester to stay on track?
- Are there any prerequisites I should be aware of?

- How can I make sure I graduate on time?
- What majors or minors align with my interests?
- How can I balance my course load more effectively?
- What resources are available if I begin to struggle academically?
- Are there opportunities I should consider, such as internships or research?

Questions to Ask Professors

Your professors are one of your most valuable resources in college. They can help you understand course material, improve your performance, and guide you toward academic and career opportunities.

Developing a relationship with your professors can also open doors to mentorship, research opportunities, and letters of recommendation.

Start by asking questions such as:

- What do successful students typically do to succeed in this course?
- How should I prepare for exams and major assignments?
- Can you clarify your expectations for this assignment?
- What study strategies do you recommend for this subject?
- Are there specific textbooks, articles, or practice materials you recommend I review?
- How can I improve my performance in this class?
- What are common mistakes students make in this course?
- Can you tell me more about opportunities in this field?
- Are there research or project opportunities I can get involved in?

Questions to Ask a Career Advisor

Career advisors help you connect your college experience to your future. They can guide you as you explore career paths, prepare for opportunities, and build the skills needed to succeed after graduation.

Meeting with a career advisor early can help you stay focused and make informed decisions throughout your college journey.

Start by asking questions such as:

- What career paths align with my interests and major?
- What internships or experience should I pursue while I am in college?
- How can I strengthen my resume and incorporate relevant experience?
- What skills are most important in my field?
- How can I prepare for career fairs and networking events?
- What should I include in my resume and cover letter?
- How can I improve my interview skills?
- What steps should I take now to prepare for my career after graduation?
- Are there specific employers or industries I should be aware of?
- How can I build a strong professional presence, including my LinkedIn profile?

Final Insight

Knowing what to ask can help you use your resources more effectively and move forward with confidence.

Successful students seek clarity, build connections, and take advantage of the support available to them.

www.ingramcontent.com/pod-product-compliance
Lightning Source LLC
LaVergne TN
LVHW041310150826
845673LV00008B/2818

* 9 7 9 8 2 1 8 6 2 1 0 2 5 *